CROCUS BOOKS

Sweet Tongues
the crocus book of food poems

ISBN 978-0-946745-78-4

First published in 2013 by Crocus
Crocus books are published by Commonword, 6 Mount Street,
Manchester M2 5NS

admin@cultureword.org.uk
www.cultureword.org.uk

Crocus books are distributed by
Turnaround Publisher Services Ltd, Unit 3, Olympia Trading Estate,
Coburg Rd, Wood Green, London N22 6TZ

Cover design by tyme design tymedesign.com
Printed by LPPS Limited www.lppsltd.co.uk

British Library Cataloguing-in-Publication Data:
a catalogue record for this book is available from the British Library.

Sweet Tongues

the crocus book of food poems

Contents

Sweet Tongues   viii
Menu   Keisha Thompson   ix

Sweet
Table In The Window   Lynn Walton   3
Fruit   Adam Lowe   4
Breakfast in Bed   Winston Plowes   5
Raspberry Fib   Shoeless Carole   6
I've got a craving   Emma Purshouse   7
In the kitchen   Almira Holmes   9
Bottled Up Jazz   Anna Percy   10
Recycled Moments   Joan Ncube   11
Dutch Pot   Yvonne McCalla   12
This England   Jolivia Gaston   13
Picnic On Wednesday   Lynn Walton   14
Sweet yu   Yvonne McCalla   16
Death By Chocolate   Neil McCall   17
Two couplets   Basir Sultan Kazmi   18
Chocolate Fingers   Katie Haigh   19
Food Is Heavenly   Tia McHale   20

Sour
Fowl Play   Hua Zi   25
The Study   Sheree Mack   26
Blending In   Charlotte Gringras   27
Home-made   Louise Fazackerley   28
Soup Kitchen   Keisha Thompson   29
Not gherkins   Shirley Percy   31
The Cake Mould   Brigid Rose   32
Coming Out   Kayleigh Kavanagh   33
Postscript   Helene Marks   34
Two Views Of Leaving   Aryamati Olga Kenyon Brooks 35
Polenta   Sarah Gbeleyi   36
In Vino Veritas   Aryamati Olga Kenyon Brooks 37
Plain Jane   Meshach R. Brencher   38
Fish Market, Orange Valley   Sheree Mack   39
Doppelgänger   Cheryl Martin   40

Bitter

Dinner at Grandma's	Reece Williams	43
Mum Says Stick Together Like Okra	Chanje Kunda	44
Dinner Party	Nadeem Zafar	45
A Taste of Marriage	Rachel Halsall	46
You Will Eat	Daniella Edwards	47
Foreboding	Keisha Thompson	48
Sweet Tooth	Elmi Ali	49
Eating The Moon	Khaleal Coleman	50
free range	Jennifer Nansubuga Makumbi	51
(Makassar) chewing like there's no tomorrow	Louise Wallwein	52
Night Owl	Gillian Forrester	53
Making a meal of it	Steve Garside	55

Salt

father cried in the kitchen	Jennifer Nansubuga Makumbi	59
The Price of Fish	Tony Walsh	60
Jamboree	Lathifa Baumgartner	61
At Gogo's house	Zodwa Nyoni	62
Sorrel wine and fish	Shirley May	63
Little Father	Elmi Ali	64
The Sandwich	SuAndi	65
Her Pot	Yusra Warsama	66
Mother B's	Shirley May	68
Dubin Coddle	Fokkina McDonnell	69
at the sandwich farmer's evening meal	conor aylward	70
Tournus	Sue Stern	71
Sunday Morning	Fokkina McDonnell	72
Joe BBQ at Barbakan	SuAndi	73

Umami

Looking for love	Hua Zi	77
Just One Monsoon	Nabila Jameel	78
Food For Life	Abi Idowu	79
Dear Future Lover	Anna Percy	83
On the origins of processed food	revporl	84
YabbY Yoods	Chris Jam	85
Sprigs of Time - Mum's Kitchen	Laura Sinclair	86
Eating for two	Almira Holmes	88

Back to Cheetham Hill, 1994   *Sue Stern*   89
Turmeric   *Nabila Jameel*   90
J. Alfred Prufrock's Last Supper *Mark Mace Smith*   92

Biographies of contributors   96

Sweet Tongues

A feast of poems featuring food

We can't live without it. From baked beans to caviar, food plays a starring role in all our lives. It not only sustains our bodies, it seeds the imaginations of poets and appears as metaphor in all the great works of literature: from the Bible's 'the bread of life' to Shakespeare's 'music be the food of love' to poet laureate Carol Anne Duffy's 'A Healthy Meal'.

History often crystallizes and preserves occasions by reference to food. Marie Antoinette is always remembered by her exclamation: 'let them eat cake!'; footballer Roy Keane captured the mood on the terraces at the time with his rail against 'the prawn sandwich brigade'; Prime Minister Margaret Thatcher will be recalled forever as the 'milk snatcher', and no memory of Henry VIII would be complete without a reference to his famous appetite for food as well as his glut of wives.

We challenged poets to write about food afresh. They have done themselves and us proud. 52 poets contributed 68 poems in five different categories: sweet, sour, bitter, salt and umami. The Contents page is your 'a la carte' for these food poems. We have also prepared some set meals for those in a hurry. Dip into the collection like tapas, or read the collection from cover to cover like a Henry VIII banquet. Either way, we hope to sate your appetite. The dinner bell is rung. Bon apetit!

MENU
by poetry chef, Keisha Thompson

Sweet
The Proof is in the Pudding
Pages 1 to 21
It would be a mistake to think of this section as a sweet nothing. There is comfort here. Honey, banana, condensed milk, fudge... and yet there is more to sweet than this.

Traced back to the Latin term *suadere* - to make something pleasant; this flavour is a verb of hedonistic proportion. Our sweet poems explore the sugary spectrum from meringue tinted elegance to jam-sandwiched innocence. Sharpen your sweet tooth and indulge.

■ ■ ■

Sour
A Fine Pickle
Pages 23 to 40
At first glance, it is easy to assume this is a nose-wrinkling section. Although derived from the Indo-European *sur* for sour milk, we can assure you these poems are still perfect for human consumption. Not all our dishes deliver acidity, fermentation or a squinted face.

Within this taste there is always room for the tart, the tangy and the zingy. Think lemon sorbet, raspberry coulis and vinegar on your chips. The poems in this section are sharp and tantalising - enjoy.

Bitter
What's Eating You?
Pages 41 to 55
The flavour that bites back - stemming from Old English
bitan. Bitter latches on to the senses and stays a while. If you
are in the mood for coffee dunked imagery and aloe musings
then take a gander. In many cultures bitter foods are valued
to maintain well-being. So have an acrid shot on us.

■ ■ ■

Salt
Salt of the Earth
Pages 57 to 74
The most versatile of the flavours, salt, a crystalline
compound of opposites. It has the potential to enhance
any dish yet too much can dry and corrode. A fisherman's
nostalgia, an onion's penchant, a fast food secret - whatever
your interpretation there will be something for you in this
section.

■ ■ ■

Umami
Uuuummmmami
Pages 75 to 94
The newest flavour to grace our menu, hailing all the way
from Japan, Oo-Ma-Me simply means "delicious". Defying
the doctrine of Democritus, the fifth flavour encompasses
the pleasure found in savoury foods. You're going to need a
napkin. These poems will have you biting your tongue in glee
and drooling like Pavlov's dogs. Sit back, undo the top button
on your jeans and don't bother asking for the dessert menu.

Meals for Two
Breakfast in Bed
Recycled Moments
Plain Jane
Looking for Love
Dear Future Lover
Yabby Yoods

Appetisers
Raspberry Fib
This England
Fowl Play
Dinner at Grandma's
You Will Eat
Makassar (chewing like there's no tomorrow)
On the Origins of Processed Food
Two Couplets

Kids Menu
Food Is Heavenly
Chocolate Fingers

From Mother's Recipe Book
Dutch Pot
Two Views Of Leaving
Mum Says Stick Together Like Okra
Foreboding
Her Pot
Mother B's
Sprigs of Time - Mum's Kitchen

Sweet

Table In The Window

Lynn Walton

my gingerbread man
straddles the coffee spoon
winking a flirty currant eye
he slides into my thoughts
the replay of his body
swirls into my cappuccino
as I move against the chair
to our night-before rhythm

the hot drinks machine sighs
I grip the table with damp fingers
as my lover hurls himself
scattering in devoted crumbs
at my feet

Fruit

Adam Lowe

You call me a fruit,
and I agree,
say

a fruit is ripe,
promising seeds,
bursting with juice.

You call me a fruit,
as though a vegetable
while I recite a litany
of fresh attributes:

a fruit is rich,
remembers its roots,
nourishes, quenches,
makes a display of any table.

I say,
I am the apple
that announces the gravity
of a given situation;
I am the pomegranate
whose gemstones teach
of the burden of possession;
I am the fig
our ancestors couldn't resist.

You call me a fruit
and I agree:
come over here
and bite me.

Breakfast in Bed

Winston Plowes

To spread myself upon you
is what I dream of most.

To gradually melt into you
like butter on my toast.

Raspberry Fib
Shoeless Carole

A
Soft
Tender
Raspberry,
Dripping sweet fresh juice,
Stimulates these moist swollen buds,
Tempts my tongue to pleasure deep in this submissive flesh.

I've got a craving

Emma Purshouse

I've got a craving
for love
as a tub of Pringles
doesn't give me tingles.
I've got a craving
for love
as a Big Mac
will not
massage my back.
I've got a craving
for love
because chips
cannot replace the brush of lips
against my skin.
I've got a craving
for love
because a chocolate éclair
will not
run its fingers through my hair.
I've got a craving
for love
as steak and kidney pies
don't look deep into my eyes
and smile.
I've got a craving
for love
as treacle pudding
won't tell me I look good in
my new dress.
I've got a craving
for love
because a full English Breakfast

doesn't leave me breathless
with desire.
I've got a craving
for love
because a kebab
even with mayonnaise on
cannot replace
a romantic liaison.
I've got a craving
for love.
I'm fed up of crumbs
in my bed,
I want a man instead.

In the kitchen
Almira Holmes

The grandfather clock strikes ten
in the other room. The sun
only shines through the window
at the solstice but the cat will
scratch the door at any time.

He stands in front of the wooden
worktop - a floured handprint
on his dark green shirt.
The fruity smell rises
through his hair as he stretches
and pummels the dough
before shaping and set it aside
to prove.

Soon the kitchen
becomes too warm and the cat
lifts its tail high and finds
somewhere soft to contemplate;
the baking bread not enough to hold
its attention.

He will be critical:
texture; too much, not enough
salt; try poppy seeds next time.

The cat smells the air, trying to catch
the hint of a hidden mouse.

Bottled Up Jazz

Anna Percy

Her head all knotted with jazz
and bread and cheese blossom scent
thinking of outmoded chrysanthemums
their frilled petals like
pastry wheels cut them
she walked disguised
pinballing street corners
in her zippered pocket

escaping the hole in the snow leopard lining
in her palm
his beloved thumb print
from last night
her synapses buzzed with extolled virtues
chronicling this dance

Recycled Moments
Joan Ncube

We spent tree swaying, wind howling,
darkness lightning, sun setting and sun rising
tangled together in love and friendship.

We spent £1.50 on our default Tesco double
choc gateau, swapping feeds
while slurping sweet chocolate flavoured kisses.

We spent moments glancing, smiling,
giggling and wallowing in a hopeful forever,
both painting our future masterpiece.

We spent time apart, thinking back,
anticipating the next time we'll spend together,
telling each other how we've missed being
tangled in love and friendship, like the last
time we met.

Dutch Pot
Yvonne McCalla

Mama, what yu cookin in yu dutch pot?
Di pot we yu fry up johnny cake,
we yu a spice we up fi tell it like it is:

Truth and lie don't mix up inna dis pot
yu a say, tell it like it is,
neva pretty it up.
Gi wi courage to walk di talk,
remind we fe give tanks fi di day
an remember
yu 'tank yu' an yu 'please'

Yu love a cook down chicken, rice an peas
fill our imagination
wid tales of Caribbean nights
when yu an' Aunty Mavis
bake yam fish an breadfruit by firelight
an pepper soup when di cold a bite

Yu flavour di whole house
wid yu salt fish and bammy

What yu cooking, nanny?

This England
Jolivia Gaston

Wednesday morning we sat opposite each other
My sisters eyes firmly on the food
She preferred her little soldiers
Toasted golden brown dipped in yellow yolk
I wanted marmalade without the pips.

Picnic On Wednesday
Lynn Walton

we meet as usual
on the neglected grass
a smudged sun glances

rags of blue
flutter between
open-armed branches

scatters of wild flowers
and a white linen square
that is our table for two

roughly chopped egg
a billow of cloud and sunshine
hugged by bread

I empty my week
you listen until
the dandelions doze

and day-end shadows
begin stretching across
our porcelain plates

cool air shifts
round my skin
nudging me back to now

I trace my finger
in the carve of your name
drop a kiss on your headstone

our house waits
its ribs scaffold
empty space

Sweet yu
Yvonne McCalla

it sweet yu
wen yu a come West Indies
sugar did sweet yu
fill up yu mansions
carve yu reputation
make yu 'leaders' of di nation
mi cyan't lie
sugar is bittersweet
remin me dat
is wi a do'it
cultivate di land
cut down di cane
wen sun a shine
an' wind bring rain
the sharpness of the cane

LORD HAV MERCY

Di rain it haard
Wen yu si yu Pitney
Sold downa market yard
While yu man a shake wid RAGE
Like a tambourine
Wen di dut it a haard
Wen massa treat mi body
Like fi him owna back yard
Wen is wi bare di scars
Dat sweeten yu tongue
Tun yu credentials into lie
How can sumbaddy
So full of knowledge
Be blind so wid two eye

Death By Chocolate
Neil McCall

Make me a cake
which will shudder my arteries
with 70 per cent cocoa,
the butter we've shunned,
white flour fit only for rats

Make me a cake
for an inbetween season
a smack in the eye
for the Puritan soul
landlording it over my body

Make me a cake
sleek-sided and wicked
deserving a fate
to be hewn into pieces
and scattered like deadly confetti

Make me a cake
which will landfill my stomach
dripfeeding cholesterol
a slice of bad fortune
depleting my life by the mouthful

Make me a cake
and we'll eat it together
when I reach expiry date
on the post-mortem
the doctor will write: "Death By Chocolate"

Two couplets
Basir Sultan Kazmi

Couplet 1
Although all those present were bitter-tongued
All of them were fond of sweets

Couplet 2

I kept waiting all night for my friends
Basir, all my cups remained unemptied

Chocolate Fingers

Katie Haigh

Sticky chocolate fingers
Messy sweet lips
Little white dress stained
With mischievous little hands
Cheeky sneaky smile
Just take a crafty bite
Mum won't notice it's gone
Until she checks the fridge tonight

Food Is Heavenly
Tia McHale (aged 11)

Some foods smell
Boys yell
Cake is nice
We eat rice
Vegetables are healthy
People are wealthy

Foods have fat
So is my cat
Foods have herbs
Like lemon curds
Spices is my mood
Food's my attitude

Lemon is yellow
Have a marshmallow
Strawberries are red
I love my bed
Apples are green
My friends lean

I love cooks
I like their looks
I drink tea
And have a wee
Customers pay
I say Yay!

I like fish
On my dish
I serve prawns
Everyone yawns
I love tomatoes on my pizza
I have a sister she's called Liza

Sour

Fowl Play
Hua Zi

Chinatown's full of ducks on hooks,
glaring at passers-by through window glass.
These, say the ducks, are our last looks
at those who'd make a meal of us.

The Study
Sheree Mack

Nobody took the time to record
the details about her.

Did she rise early and collect
eggs from the yard?
Or did she rest in till late?

Did she nudge her hips into
the bench while kneading dumplings?
Or did she buy them in?

Would she sit some evenings, alone,
darkness here in the blink of an eye
and she still waiting?

One question leads to another.

Flowers - did she love them?
The fat trumpeting heads
of the hibiscus cover her
in the Master's surviving studies.

In the final painting,
she is gone, replaced by
a mountain in the distance.

Blending In
Charlotte Gringras

Friends went home to hot cross buns
when I went back to *kichels*; I longed
to share those buns' religious connotations -
forbidden to, I'd make tasty imitations.
I couldn't bake a gooey Christmas cake
lest mimcry of Christian friends would make
me less Jewish. Yet more like them I yearned
to be - then they'd like me. Maybe they'd spurn
the New Year honey cake I brought, trying
to win them over, constantly vying
with them to reach their uniformity
of food to share, aspiring to conformity.
My *Pesach* cookies went down a treat
serving only to set me apart, to separate;
to join the fold it took pancakes on a plate
sugar-sprinkled, shared for Shrove Tuesday.
Provided that we called it Pancake Day
I could belong; join the gang, play the game
feel like everyone and almost be the same.

Home-made

Louise Fazackerley

Static sheets in a posh hotel,
a 'one year anniversary' mix CD
and a cupcake with a candle
saying 'LOVE FROM ME'

I baked home-made sponge with jam
for your Mam, when we lodged with her.
You skated on the thin white icing that I tried to hide
with sugar hearts and chocolate flakes and hugs.
When I shouted 'Surprise' she cried.
I didn't know then the way you talk to her,
the way you sweeten her with lies.

Warm sheets in a rented flat,
anniversary fleas from next-door's cat,
and a bun in the oven.
No room for words.

Now there's nothing left in the joint account
and your child wants and wants and wants
a Disney Princess supermarket cake.
I invite a pay day loan to the party-
1383 % interest with a cherry on top.
The kids stuff and fizz until they pop
while you watch TV.
You have 0% interest in her or me.

Dirty laundry washed in the street,
I hired a man complete with a van
but we can't lift the cooker between us.

Soup Kitchen
Keisha Thompson

Lyard boots by the door,
a home-less man in the kitchen

Lionised by large pieces of yam,
cassava and halal chicken

Diginity is folded neatly,
tucked into the breast-pocket of nostalgia

His beard is bruque,
his feet are cleaner than a prophet's

Behind his heels,
a bag of jeans for darning

She will find they are beyond repair,
buy three new pairs from Ethel Austin

In front of the hob, half oracle, half slave
she cleaves a nullified contract

In the bubbling nostrum we swell
towards one another like poaching bagels

Before we cloy, he laces his boots
and stutters his way to the door

She says: Good night Mr Thompson
before I can figure out what to say

Good night Dad
Good night Father
Good night Daddy

The pale brown rimmed bowl
is returned to the cupboard.

Not gherkins
Shirley Percy

A post war, working class child,
chewing my way through sameness,
if I thought of them at all,
it was as weird green things
in the mixed pickles jar
with its stark vinegar stink.

In France, on exchange,
I found my railwayman's family
eating like kings. Noticing my smile,
at dinner he pushed across
unidentified delights in sauces
tasting of sunny fields, deep woods.
"The Anglaise eats well." I relished
The *cornichons'* sharp come-hither taste,
flirting with many flavoured cheeses.
From the top shelf came
a huge jar; preserved cherries.
I said I loved their liquid.
A belly laugh. To Madame's horror
he offered me absinthe.
I slept most of next day.

Back in England,
meeting that strange word *gherkin*
I found it foreign, meaningless.
Cornichon had resonances
Of family life and laughter.

To me, they were never gherkins.

The Cake Mould
Brigid Rose

When I met you I bought a bra -
cream lace arranged around
a wire frame - to form and flatter
womanhood. To present me more pleasingly.
To construct me less crudely.

Putting it on, concealing it under clothes
to say a secret, *Eat me, love* -
I made a cake of myself for you, frilling
myself up like a frothy thing to be
undone, in the hope I'd not be left-overs.

You undressed me (bra pulled
hurriedly over head, you did not
unfasten) and said, *shall I eat her
with cream or custard?*
I let you help yourself to everything.

Now I don't see you but I wear the bra.
I am an adorned thing, uselessly,
straps digging my skin
where I puddinged when you left.

Coming Out
Kayleigh Kavanagh

Peeling away the layers,
    my beauty brought tears
to your
       eyes

    bruise coloured skin
    a shelter,
cut through, touchable,
    tasteable,
       breakable

       dug up too early, picked
       too late

Postscript
Helene Marks

Abandoning the balsamic and the extra virgin
cold pressed, I boiled 2 eggs.

Everything happens in those years of growing up.
Everything else is a postscript.

Flung out into the world half cooked, you run away
with yourself until the yolk of you hardens,

the membrane thins, the calcified shell of you arrives
back at the beginning and soft boiled eggs suffice.

Two Views Of Leaving

Aryamati Olga Kenyon Brooks

When he stamped off, she offered no resistance,
just spread all Yorkshire on her table,
prepared and cooked it at her leisure,
dreamed it, kissed it; presented it to herself

then made us parkin, rich with syrup and raisins.
Oblivious, we ran out to play
leaving her to speak only to the room he'd loved.

She washed the dishes, as shiny as her eyes;
years later when we slunk home, we saw her sunken cheeks.
She surrounded us with wrist and forearm -
we fled; she seldom spoke again.

Polenta
Sarah Gbeleyi

Corn, deafened, beaten, smashed, wind-thrashed,
fire blazed through metallic sheets, ground to grit,
left to rest encased in plastic,

> drought dry and parched for preservation,
> no reservation, walk-in orders taken:
> in minutes boiled, cooled, grilled...

Savour the taste, meek and mild in flavour, humbly
mopping up rich sauces, yet itself a source of wealth
men barter daily, unbeknown to bride:

call it dowry, commodity, futures, and yet before
the baby's head is wet, its future is bet, the price is set,
before the screams, before even the labour it seems:

> food for thought, for biofuel, for fodder
> for scraps sold as meal, now, which seems odder?

my multiple needs for a replanted seed, to feed livestock,
birds, economies - I give it value, irrespective of whether I value
it

Though I do, I value its humility, its history, its beauty,
I value its vivid yellow hue, its simple texture, its palatable shine

> And when I serve it up, I know
> in secret, I've eaten gold.

In Vino Veritas

Aryamati Olga Kenyon Brooks

The second bottle tastes better than the first. It's
midnight, left his wife screaming in childbirth at home.
He gets up to welcome a shy blonde at the bar;
she turns him down.

Safer to sit, he feels a gentle sadness
emanate, orders a third bottle;
a shifting of gears, at the next gulp
he settles wife and boys in France,
boss disappears, he bulldozes all the worst slums;
makes a great speech, doubles everyone's salary.

Slowly the walls fade under the influence of a cool waltz.
He slips to the ground and lies there, happy as the dead.

Plain Jane
Meshach R. Brencher

I kiss her once and I kiss her again, then again and again
but she doesn't want me eating her face off
take it easy babe she says, save it for later on, I'm fine for now
she is plain Jane, plain Jane

I want to make her dinner and use my recipe of love
to tantalise her taste buds, cook her something special
just how she makes me feel, she says, don't go to that effort
forget the roast, just serve me up beans on toast
she is plain Jane, plain Jane she really is

Fish Market, Orange Valley

Sheree Mack

Changing from one moment to the next moment,
the skins of red fish had too many colours to choose.
Early morning they'd be
thrashing in pod nests, their eyes
fixed marbles where the sea once rode.

The men, in net vests and shorts,
stroked the fish with a cool, practiced passion.
And before each gleaming body
they'd be on their knees, claiming
their riches from the seas.

In wanting-light, small boats moored,
fish, men and sea would retreat
into the arms of women.

Doppelgänger
Cheryl Martin

Ten years isn't long enough.
I look for you in my mirror
to see if you marked me
(to kiss dry ice -
to love you).

Vichyssoise,
red caviar,
champagne -
scissors down my throat.
You ruined my appetite
because you couldn't eat.

Evensong,
madrigals,
crying in the chapel.
Brown-skin girls bruise, too.
I learned that from you.

Ten years isn't long enough to forget:
I look for you in my mirror
in terror
someone will see
that once we were the same.

(To kiss dry ice -
to love you).

Bitter

Dinner at Grandma's

Reece Williams

We trust each other
Everywhere else
But here;
Say our grace
With open eyes.

Mum Says Stick Together Like Okra
Chanje Kunda

You are doing what?
You met a guy in a nightclub once
Sent a couple of emails and now you are going
To fly back to see him?
See that picture there of sliced tomatoes,
Red and shining with juice,
Ripened by the sunshine
Full of all that is good for you;
That is what family is.

He could chop you up into little pieces
We eat tilapia, green vegetables,
Pounded maize meal, inshima is bubbling,
Until it becomes firm as the family bond.
I don't understand what you are running away from.
Yes life is hard, being a mother is hard,
But we stick together like okra.

And by the way,
Smoking Ganja is not African.
No self-respecting African woman does that.
The pots and pans
Are cooking places for
Love brewed in an African pot.
What do you hope to get from going to Amsterdam?
I worked all my life and want to see you doing well,
I didn't work 2 jobs to bring you up
So you could end up in Amsterdam on drugs
Why can't you date that nice Zambian boy I introduced you to?

Dinner Party
Nadeem Zafar

August 1991

The film was about to start when
my phone went off. "You're needed here," she said.

I got back and filed into the kitchen. Mum passed plates.
As I took my first mouthful of rice and dahl, Dad blurted it out:

"You have another sister."
He kept eating as he told us. I almost choked.

I chewed relentlessly, but the grains of rice stayed tasteless,
the dahl stiff in my mouth.

Dad gazed at me in sadness.
I got up from the table.

A Taste of Marriage

Rachel Halsall

Put down the paper, you have already made
A braille of bruises to read over breakfast
Burned as it lies, like my hand, too long under the grill
So I bind black pudding in bandages
And count each eggshell fragment in the X ray
Each crumb of toast spat into the sink
An unwritten tabloid headline
On the double page
Of my rib cage
Don't check the timer, there is no need to wait
For the crimson kettle to come to the boil
Turning to nurse a tender turkey breast beneath its
Tight wrap of white tape and sticky plasters
A week, and still not ready to take
Out to the tabletop where the
Soup spoils from the spill of salt
Or blood that won't show
In tomato

You Will Eat
Daniella Edwards

He sat me there, I was three or four
And I had to eat what he'd cooked.
Mum was in a chair in a corner, upset.
I didn't want to eat it. He insisted.
It was a battle of wills - nothing
To do with food.
Mum cried. I ate. He sighed.

Foreboding
Keisha Thompson

I

She said she dreamt fish -
live fish!
Stood in the market eyeing up
Snapper, Bangamary and Trout
on one side,
Houri, Patwa and Hassa
on the other.

My sister and I exchange glances,
like sisters do.

To an outsider this is that mundane
morning talk, between opening
the fridge aimlessly, then on the
third attempt grabbing the milk.

II

Every child in this family had been pre-empted
by her otherworldly trips to the fish market.
Last time, Aunty called to share the good news -
If it comes from anyone else it is good news.

As I pray for the phone to ring
my sister asks what it means if you dream
dead fish? What if you dream that you scaled it,
chopped its head off and fried it in oil?

Sweet Tooth
Elmi Ali

She stopped in front of the fridge, caught her breath. Hiked up her *abaya*, spread her legs, and sat. Enjoying the cold of the trazel floor seeping through her underwear, cooling both cheeks evenly.

With her palms, she rubbed the place in her inner thigh where she'd just removed the needle; replaced the vial of insulin between the custard and condensed milk. And decided to sit for a while. Half of her face glowing, set alight by the open fridge.

Eating The Moon
Khaleal Coleman

He sways into the room
A waterfall of slurs and grunts
His eyes filled with the secrets of his heart

He has uncorked the bottle
The crops of awareness washed away
These floods will become tides
He will never be moonwise.

free range
Jennifer Nansubuga Makumbi

the hotel door was a shell, it cracked at his knock. inside the wall was white smooth. breakfast rolled clean on the plate from one end to another. he smelt neither protein nor cholesterol.

in the bubbling heat, the last hopes of a cluckling mother had been dashed. her loss was his gain.

with both hands, he pressed hard. the walls, squidgy, tore away. he liked them hard boiled. but the sun that emerged was soft. it shuddered a bit, spilled, and ran. peeling his appetite with it.

(Makassar) chewing like there's no tomorrow
Louise Wallwein

The herds have come to love the taste of sweet wrappers.

Chewing like there's no tomorrow
their patches evolve
no need to brand them anymore,
golden arches grow on their backs instead.

Night Owl
Gillian Forrester

I saw a fox at 2am -
I'd been wakened by the smell of coffee
and the sound of scraping toast,
the hint of blackened bread.
In flats like these,
Seventies built, with concrete corridors,
the breeze of other lives through the walls
and ventilation from below,

slow cooking casseroles vying for air space
with mint shampoo and Alep soap -
but now it's 2am and a fox is sniffling outside.

My neighbour needs the night noises
which bring her sleep;
the click of snooker balls, the strident last order calls,
the desperate final fling on the fruit machine.
Crazy serenades, lullabies mapping a lifetime.

Landladies eat at midnight, put up their feet
and wait. Her body clock refuses
to accept retirement and now it's 2am
and her legs are restless, her mind still listening
to the soothing music of endless sporting
conversations, needing the smoke,
her fruitless diet sabotaged
by dead of morning buttered toast.

The darkness shows differences, changes
morality, confuses the eye about the safety of light.
You hear a different voice in the night, when
Glenmorangie is drunk easily and without guilt.

The fox moves suddenly, quickly along the cutting,
once a filed track but now a footpath.
Telepathically, supernaturally it knows the old way.

Making a meal of it
Steve Garside

We sit in an ecstasy of kitchen scents;
jasmine by the window ledge suggests

late summer somewhere else -
somewhere we once owned a postcard from,

a place where we learned this recipe;
stumbled over the pronunciation

of vowel sounds and fricatives;
loving the swallowing of something

new; fresh as mushrooms
teased from mountain earth

then chopped into simmering oil;
the crush of a clove of garlic

refreshing the elegance of leaves
we trailed with echoes of bells on the breeze,

before the diagnosis of days so numbered,
and you cutting up my food for me.

Salt

father cried in the kitchen

Jennifer Nansubuga Makumbi

i watched him peel the thin dried layers first. purple husks, streaked with darkness lie on the side of the chopping board.

mother buys them on purpose, the fiery purple ones. bulby tight layers of malice. he cuts the pouting top first, then the roots, then the middle. two halves fall on either side of his knife, dancing with glee. he sniffs.

one half diced, his hands rise to his face, rubbing the first tears from his eyes. still he chops, along and across, blinking rapidly. he has taken most of it when the knife falls and he runs past, blind. crying.

The Price of Fish
Tony Walsh

Expert hands grip the ropes
and lower now
as one.

Rough thumbs rub at
salted tears,
or pull at collars, tighter
than the last time.

A strong wind,
uninvited, mocks
and flaps at coats
and push-chairs.

And the ocean swells
like a widow's throat.
And the ocean swells
like a mother's pain.
And the ocean swells
like a comrade's fear.

And later,
when the tea and the whiskey
and the smoke and the ham
have sunk without a tasting,

voices rage and voices hush,
voices rage and voices hush,
voices rage and voices hush

to discuss the price of fish.

Jamboree

Lathifa Baumgartner

On a seafood platter
hissing, the sting ray
dressed in sweet-sour sauce,
a sprinkling of golden pineapple
in tiny cubes,
strips of green capsicum
and small onions white as pearls,
reminiscent of colourful gems
on a red sandy beach

four large king prawns
sizzling on metal skewers
their tails fanning out
like frills on a child's frock

besides freshly-ground chillies
and a dash of lemongrass,
panache on crystal glass plates -
a choice of steamed jasmine or saffron rice,
the sweet juice of young coconuts
in their hard shells

bring to mind a garden party
mother hosted on my twenty-first
birthday, satisfying the appetite
of family and friends.

At Gogo's house
Zodwa Nyoni

In the township of Nkulumane we ate with our hands.

Watched her cook mealie-meal over an electric two plate stove.
Slowly she would sprinkle *vuvuzela,*
Letting the pounded corn meal fall between her fingers
Into the pot, thickening the mixture.
When ready, she'd dish the meal, *isitshwala,* into communal
bowls.

uKhulu would give grace of thanks and love.
Together, we'd pick sticky segments, roll them with our fingers
To dip in plates of fried spring greens, mopane worms,
Okra and stewed beef.

Supper at grandmother's house was eaten
Whilst sat on woven straw mats laid on concrete kitchen floors.

As we pulled our fingers back from our lips, *Gogo* would smile
Saying "*Abantwana babantwa bami,* children of my children.
This is how I raised your mother, eat plenty and be well."

Sorrel wine and fish

Shirley May

He spoke of sorrel wine and fish on a Friday,
of rice and peas, his mother's - our grandmother's -
sweet potato pudding, his knowledge of cricket
and Sir Garfield Sobers.

He spoke of dancing to John Holt on a Saturday night,
brandy shorts and Guinness, holding his woman right,
and how it reminded him of home: of jukeboxes, reggae
and mento music vibrating off roof tops,
the blessed assurance that came from the churches
on every street corner, and listening to Jim reeves
on a Sunday.

There were times life and love treated him hard
in this cold place. He said try to be who you are,
be true to yourself - it's what was taught him,
it was his philosophy. Even if life punched ugly wounds.

So he cooked and he played and he danced
to his own rhythms. In those movements
his children were conceived.

Little Father
Elmi Ali

On the first day of spring -
when the sun forgets about being proper
and curls its once stiff upper lip, into a scorching smile -

He gets off the bus two stops early.
A small bottle of sweetener -
like a cow bell -
in his breast pocket.

Walks into my house unannounced
and downs a glass of water.

~~

Last winter - with my father's
gait - he strolled into a ward,
scattered his things neatly on a bedside table;

before an abscess was drained.

One month later, stirring
two small tear drops into his tea,
He confessed:

"*Abo*, this thing is killing me."

The Sandwich
SuAndi

Part of her enjoys the ritual
An opportunity to meet and greet old friends
To feel the warmth of a family
Extended into a community holding hands
Linking the past to the present
Ancestors watching rituals

Trepidation lay only in timing
Not the cynicism of
Black people are always late
But the eulogies, tears, hymns, prayers
And always the preaching

She thinks
If I hear 'Amazing Grace' one more time
I will die!
Still she sings
Though sometimes she mimes the odd verse with a purpose
A signifier of a too long farewell
No disparagement to the tearful grief of sadness
Simply meeting the need of her belly
She always arrives prepared
The four-quarter substances
Of a corn beef sandwich
Which she swallows invisibly
With every Amen

Her Pot
Yusra Warsama

Cook it up, cook it up
Like I cooked you in my pot

That's what she would say

On the mountain top which once my youthful mind could
climb, where I would imagine touching clouds, finding comfort
where reality's love presides

Now the clouds are nothing but what we are told they were:
precipitation lingering in my palm

Her palm was aged before she cut her second set of teeth, aged
from washing pots in nomadic lands
Now in the Empire's homeland she would smile and say

Cook it up, cook it up,
In your pot place the things you need then add in abundance
things you think you might not

Cook it up, cook it up
Thoughts of her move me away from the false stuff that tastes
good

Glutton for punishment when it comes to feeding knowledge
The knowledge I was told so piously to seek

Cook it up, cook it up
Like I cooked you in my pot

Fool for love when it comes to matters of the heart, my belly
somersaults with the accusation from a false inner voice
Not mine
Not hers

Cook it up, Cook it up,
Place nothing but love in our pot

Mother B's
Shirley May

People love her cornmeal porridge, 2 hour dumplings,
Stew peas and rice,
      her salt pork on their lips.

Mother B's Irish Moss and Guinness punch came
with a warning, helped a brother to kiss right,
      rented rooms for the night.

She descends into the cellar, turns on the red light,
sets up the bar for the night. Her house was the spot
      after the Reno was shut.
People come from far and wide to sway, Persian
de music man play John Holt: Cupid, draw back your bow,
      you know love will find a way.

Mother B tells us stories of St Mary, where mi poppa's
people deh come from: Obia men, women who practice science
yet still fear God, Anansi's cunning; whilst remembering
the quiet place up the hill, the burying ground,
      where the nutmeg tree shades.

She whispers her memory in my ear,
descends into the cellar, turns on the red light,
sets up the bar for the night. Her house was the spot
      after the Reno was shut.
People come from far and wide to sway, Persian
de music man play Jimmy Cliff: Many rivers to cross,
      reminder of home.

Dublin Coddle
Fokkina McDonnell

Saturday supper is a savoury stew.
Sausages, and slices of bacon.
Potatoes and onion supplanted
the oatmeal and leek. Enough stock

to barely cover, season to taste,
simmer slowly, let the liquid reduce.
Tears run down the steamy window.
Chopping parsley holds the pain.

One of us poured a steady Guinness;
the other already lost in the black
and salty taste of waiting.
Between us the open cookery book:

a small black and white picture,
North Earl Street, Dublin, 1904.
Blurred images of men in coats
and caps, horse-drawn cart, a sunny day.

A couple crosses the tramlines.
He carries bags in both hands.
She, to the right of him,
looks down to safely place her feet.

at the sandwich farmer's evening meal

conor aylward

my peat infested claw digs in,
at the softest thing its touched all day,
two spongy wads of sliced pan.
gripped between me fingertips, all raw with wounds.

the sandwich chewed, rolled from side to side,
lavished a heaven on the taste buds,
all dried from black dusted air.

I felt no need to speak.
the softness of the silence was all I desired,
as to each, in turn, I nodded and smiled.
each of us recounting sods turned
and cider money honest earned.

Tournus

Sue Stern

I'll remember Tournus
for the rum and raisin ice cream
I ate at the pavement café
of the Hotel St Philibert.

Across the way, the Abbaye bells
tolled to the residents.
They waited for the English to fall
from the Route du Soleil, spend

euros on pork sausage, pâté,
and mini leek quiches from the freezer.
The purple sky leaned on the poplars
edging the Saone and became yellow

over the camp site. Lightning
forked for hours but no rain fell.

he eggs with cold water.
Do it quickly. A dog or a cat
for egg cup? You choose.
(The dog has a blue eye.
Sulphur yellow and spiteful
black make up the cat's
colour spectrum.) Just now
Joyce Carol Oates spoke
on *Private Passions* of her love
of Chopin and her interest
in boxing. Boxing has a history,
she said and, just like music,
you learn more from a replay.
It was an old city where that other
poet sat, coolly cracking
the egg of a fine Leghorn chicken.
Venice? Rhodes?
You tell me the title,
I'll give you the last line:
Surely we have....
No! Don't start that again.

Joe BBQ at Barbakan

SuAndi

Stacking shelves
Is norm to shop life
The smell of bread filling the nostrils
Hundreds of branches away from the masses of Tesco
Here fresh comes each morning
As customers, cluck their approval
In voices local to Warszawa Krosno, Kraków
And children arrive in carriages of splendour
To advertise tastelessly their parents social standing
He is bright, affable always happy
A boy in a man doing tasks that have no need of thought
But its clear he's thinking
Planning a future just a degree away
Promotion comes clouded
The shop warm from baker's oven
Pushes him outside into the daily chill of Manchester
And the pungency of onions waiting death on the grill
At first he simply toils
Dashing in, out back and forth
Remembering and forgetting
First the ketchup, napkins, waste bins
But as weeks pass and winter departs
The sun comes out to twin the brightness of his spirit
Now he stands tall in his own Kingdom
A professional at the barbecue
He speaks of ingredients laying out his taste preferences
Bratwurst or frankfurters, over the spice of chorizo
He is the greeter of every customer
Grinning warmly like the best of hosts

He has found his calling
There is an art to what he does
But the prospects are limited
And he has designs on so much more

In 2012 Joseph Hartley was named New Designer of the Year at the New Designers graduate show in London.

Umami

Looking for love
Hua Zi

Chinese woman. Unimportant fact: a real *non-looker*.
But with a heart warm as steamed flour-blankets
ready to wrap up crispy aromatic duck;
with a character spicy as SiChuan Ma-Po tofu
soft in texture but has a lasting tang on the tongue;
with a mind complicated as sweet and sour sauce
not sure whether sugar or vinegar making it tick.

To answer this honest ad,
pen a piquant verse about yourself.

Just One Monsoon
Nabila Jameel

It is our last meal and almost time to leave.
Seconds tick as loud as the Azaan;
the house is full like a mosque in the evening.

We swallow lumps of memories
with every morsel, each bite delicious
and never-ending, like the opening meal of a fast.

Later, at the airport,
I fill my eyes with your countenance —
sustenance for the next eight seasons.

*Azaan: call to prayer

FOOD FOR LIFE: RECIPES ON HOW TO CATCH AND LOSE A MAN IN SEVERAL PLATES/MENUS/DISHES
Abi Idowu

Two things Mother Dea taught me
Two things for sure she claimed
The first; a man can live and die by food
And the second, how to cook.

It's a hard, hard road for a single girl
A lonely hard, long road
Many a single, lonely hard-done girl
Will find some comfort in food.

Recipe One: 'All Alone Rice Réchauffer'. Serves One.

Take some left over boiled rice in a pan, slice and fry a fresh tomato, a medium onion, half a scotch bonnet, a red bell pepper in tinned sardines' oil. Season with one stock cube. Mix in the left over rice and serve. Have a large glass of white wine; eat as the salt of your tears mingles with your rice. Eat alone.

"Mother Dea says 'there's nothing sadder (more lonely) than a 3 day pyjamas'ed girl eating 'I'm all alone rice'."

Moving on. Sometimes a man gets his loving right and his Woman feels so right. She feels like a queen and wants to adore Him. So she strokes his head lying on her perfumed lap, singing Him songs of well fed and loved men gone by.

Recipe Two: (The Lullaby of) 'He Loves Me Right Combo'. Serves Two People Who Are Now One.

Get prime cuts of lamb and beef, also chicken breasts and cut in big cubes. Braise in butter, then add chopped carrots, shredded green cabbage leaves, a clove of garlic, a cup of sweet corn, a cup of sweet Ramiro pepper, a deseeded scotch bonnet, a large onion chopped and 1½ cups of okra/lady fingers chopped, stirring gently while you hum. Season to taste then add if you wish, ½cup king prawns, ½cup of oysters, ½ cup mussels and ½cup crab meat. Then squeeze in a ½teaspoon of lime to reduce the slime and cook for 15 minutes. Serve on a warm bed of rice and very cold lemonade to drink as you sit together, eating, smiling and filing the lovely moments away in your minds.

"Mother Dea says 'when man love woman right, she got to show pleasure, so she take the love and stir it up in the kitchen, make a man stomach proud and hard.'"

Betrayal. After giving a heart to a man and he goes on
To cheat; there's only one way to deal. Into the
Kitchen and whatever comes out can determine
His health or death.

Recipe Three: Recipe for The 'Why? Aka How Could You? Flan'. Serves One Disrespectful Undeserving Man

Take the man's favourite fruit and boil with sugar to make syrup. Make a sweet pastry case. Ground up 4 heavy duty constipation tablets, mix with the fruit syrup and fill the pie. Then bake for 10 minutes and serve with ice-cream or custard. Rubbing his arm as he eats sheepishly not daring to ask why the pie tastes funny. Smile as you

foresee him run.

"Mother Dea thinks 'woman who cooks flan for cheating man might have a plan which likely end him up bad.'"

Recipe Four: 'Cheating Bastard Aka He's Dead to Me' Hotpot. Serves One Cheating Bastard

Get every low end part of meat and fish, for example, offal, gills, bones etc and boil them together with salt and 2 large scotch bonnet pepper. Make a well salted short crust pastry seasoned with chilli flakes in one hotpot mould. Fill the mould with the mix, cover with a short crust top and seal, bake for 30 minutes and serve with a fork while you sit holding the knife (make sure it's a steak knife) watching him. When he chokes, never leave your seat, nor let him leave his.

"Mother Dea warns 'cheating bastard who survives hotpot, either hand over will or make peace with God, cos one thing's for sure, when mad wife is done; either he die or live.'"

When all that is done, its time for sorrow to be gone
Time to take a shower and wash your hair
Shave your legs, wear a pretty dress and
Have a 'breathing free' celebration trifle
No trifling, it's all for yourself.

Recipe Five: 'Breathing Free Celebration Trifle'. Serves One Life Survivor.

Go out to the best cake store in town and buy yourself your favourite fruit sponge cake or if you'd rather, make one. Also get or make some contrasting fruit jelly (for example strawberry sponge, orange jelly) and cream.

Go home. Get a trifle bowl and cut the cake into four
pieces. Line the bowl with two pieces of the cake, pour
over half the jelly and cover the top with some cream.
Repeat and set in the fridge to chill. Set the table, put
some flowers in a vase, get the cake, seat yourself down,
breathe deep and eat.

*"Mother Dea says 'once in a while, when girl's heart broke, girl need
love herself and cake is love. She breathe free and then decide if she
need improve on 'all alone rice' or start practising 'the yam pottage'
again.'"*

PS: No man died in the creating of this poem.

Dear Future Lover,

Never say "You can't quit me, baby," for you are unlikely to be
American or an opiate. I do not want or need you to promise
to be there until the final furlong, such binds fail to understand
how much luck is apportioned to each of us and how chance
can laugh at your plans. I have never eaten red peaches, I like
to imagine they taste different to white or flat; stronger. We
could watch each other become vampired by sweetness. I would
like you to make me unafraid to walk the paths of slaves into
the Aquaducts. If you can find romance on Lynwood Avenue
you can find it anywhere, this is required. If you can be a solid
phantom I will welcome you. Here, when you leave a place by
road, the name appears again crossed through, as if it no longer
exists for you.

Patiently Yours,

Anna Percy

On the origins of processed food
revporl

A great man,
Had a big plan,
He said, hey man,
Canned spam!

YabbY Yoods
Chris Jam

Let's sit still...chill....if your will wills let's talk.......let's break
unleavened bread.......palpating pittas..... cascading comfort
conjuring chapattis....contagious croissants..... will waking
wholegrain....... wholly processed Loafs...... Hard Dough... Soda
bread... Let's talk YabbY Yoods

Let's countenance balance.......we've been foolishly nurtured
to fiend on an over prevalence of protein since our ancestors
admirable adventurousness led them to relegate balanced
harmonious sustainable agricultural pursuits..........

Let's incite innovation.... imbibe inspiration....expire
eviscerating............enshrine Eating education...........
creAte collective Celebrations.........Foods facilitation......
harmonization of families....streets......neighbourhoods.....
communities...whole wholesomely bestowed.....by that which
when unencumbered.....un-tampered enhances folks.....the
Spokes of the wheels.....that are Humanity's gears.....the food
the fuel for the engine room of....imagination......of nations.

Simple solution... we need a RevoFooDtion!

Sprigs Of Time - Mum's Kitchen

Laura Sinclair

Mr Brown melts away the whiteness of bland meat
   Aroma dances through the house like a
      Babalawo evoking orishas from the deep
         Scented waved steps she gives colour to the colourless

   Black and white fireplace
   black and white settees, T.V. screens

Living room alive with the sizzle, low hums hissing
   All purpose spiced-licked chicken
      Heat, oil, pan, tomatoes, onion and garlic
       Mutton simmering
         Something cooking
           Food deh pon di fire

Sprigs of thyme separate the present and chase minds into
                       recline
   Into memories further back into histories of ours, ingrained
      In blood lines passed down through time
         We find ourselves in these recipes

Gregory's baseline married mum's off key humming tide
   And gave birth to her swaying waistline
      Bottomless earth tones tease out in steam clouds
         Bubbles hurried and spoon beats chimed at black
                  dutchy's side
      The melody of blue and orange dancing flames
                 underneath
  Spoke silently and played games, heat

The matrimony of fire and pot housed laughter
Thick baritones and singing Creole wove our spirits tighter
Whilst Scotch bonnet licked taste buds satisfied bellies
United, we eat.

Slow, steady rhythm in her heel toe
She goes to and fro with afro head scarfed
Between hands placed either side of Jamaica tray
Lay humbly black generations on a white plate
Djembe thumbed in her chest
Basket on her head

She returned to bring come another plate.

Eating for two
Almira Holmes

My ante-natal card stands brightly against the clock.
The breakfast egg has the texture of shoe-leather.
I dab cold tea behind my ears thinking, this is Chanel No. 5.
Good news - I have achieved *my* desired weight.
Bad news - there's seven months to go before it'll be that again.
I paint the nursery a delicate shade of lilac.

The apricot jam sandwich tastes of rusty corned beef.
I flush 29 iron pills down the loo.
My taste buds zing as I spread gorgonzola on a ginger biscuit.
I blanket stitch a hole in the top of a crimson bell-tent.
Despite increasing girth, I'm invisible on buses and trains.
Feeling good, I take down and wash all the curtains.

Heartburn doesn't stop me spreading Piccalilli on my cheese
                                                    sandwich.
I find my blood pressure's up and I receive a stern warning.
Although I take a pee every five minutes my bladder still leaks.
The house shudders when I climb the stairs.
The dog-eared ante-natal card has fallen behind the clock.

Back to Cheetham Hill, 1994
Sue Stern

Today, at the Halal meat and fruit, a man swings from a car.
Tall, fearless, gold glittering waistcoat, he feints a blow. The
shopkeeper ducks. They disappear, leaving melons, mulis, yams
and aubergines.

Long ago, after pictures at *The Greenhill,* we walked home eating
chips. 'Have some, pet, your dad won't know.' Mary, my friend's
mum, died five years ago, sucking out her heart on Craven A.
We learned of love reading her *Woman's Weekly* on wet Sundays.

I edge my way now through the village. *Sheitels* sleek as bowls,
women push prams and chat, daughters dawdling, frilled cuffs
pointing and squealing at dogs. Men run, string laddered *tsitsit*
swinging beneath dark coats. Eyes elsewhere, a man drops
change into my palm, avoiding female touch.

English, Yiddish, Croat, Hindi, Irish blurred by traffic. David at
The Laughing Lentil, speaking some of each, sings them arias from
The Gondoliers.

And my mother. Her story penned in careful copperplate, peeks
from the plastic bag; her coat slung over a chair. 'Come on,' I call,
'your car awaits. Leave them to the cheese and raisins.'

Turmeric
(For Kobab Jameel, may you rest in peace)
Nabila Jameel

The little loops in your Rs
make me smile
as I skim labels on jars
in your cupboard:

'Garam Masala'
'Meat Tenderiser'

You, rushing about from cooker
to sink, from cupboard to table.
Neglected peels on a newspaper.
The smells of new recipes,
unknown flavours, bottles of fizz,
steam on the window.

That old tea towel with fading herbs.
Hot ladles of chatter warming our plates
as the sun closes its eyes.

I turn one jar of turmeric
to see the whole label,
yellowed by the rush
of your fingertips,
and jaundice in your eyes.

Touching the label
I think of your gravestone,
then holding the jar, your coffin.

It's as if in mid-chore, while stirring,
you went to answer the phone
but forgot to come back;
as if these jars are waiting
for your return.

J. Alfred Prufrock's Last Supper
Mark Mace Smith

Let us eat then, you and I -
Come die with me ... dine
A hippy hot pot of the nouveaux kind served upon a half-
deserted table
Let us eat, forget the cupcake dessert or the restorative bedtime
Bovril
All from now will be inedible, these Piscean portions of Yin and
Yang
may look in their symmetry as fine dining
yet these limp soggy flowers will be the death of us

In the kitchen the women come to gasp and gas
Talking of the death of Sylvia Plath

The yellowed petals of limpid Lilliputian lilianas
lingered in the pools upon the plate
they let fall their moist stamens,
let fall their flower bells that once rung out and sprung up in
splendid grace,
wilted in a wind that shed all of their pollen and most of their
beauty,
prepared and curled upon a dinner plate to herald us to heaven's
gate

And indeed there will be time
for the customary after dinner smoke
grey green limp wisps waiting to be wafted, whipped by the
wind
towards the yellow fogged window panes
There will be time, there will be time
to prepare our bodies to meet the faces of those who will find us
There will be time to consider murder, suicide and the creative

urge to destroy
Time for all the quaint ways of our lives to be seen in our
vision,

flashed before our eyes without revision
There may be time for a cup of tea, coffee or a brandy
but there will be no time for inhibition, ices or cake

In the kitchen the women come to gasp and gas
Talking of the death of Sylvia Plath

And indeed there will be time
to wonder "Do I care?" and "Do I care?"
but no time to turn back and descend the stair
this rub-a-dub-grub of a diet will make us quiet
no more evenings, mornings, afternoons measured out with
crack spoons
this evening we will sleep so peacefully, eternally,
turning our masculine and feminine living energy into a eulogy
to our memory
(They will say: how could they commit this sin?)

And how should I presume?
Do I care? And will I make a great cadaver, brown and bare?
(But in the lamplight, downed with light white hair!)
As I lie with this pillow by my head, stretched on the floor,
you here beside me, you elegant with your shawl
our breath scuttling towards dead shores and dead pauses and
dead silent seas.
(They will say: He is not Lazarus, he will not come back from
this deep)

And would it have been worth it, after all,
After all the marshmallows, the fish pies, the tea
among the Elizabethan porcelain and the hovering kingfishers

among positive and negative talk of you and me
would it have been worthwhile? Or just disappointing?

No! I am not Prince Hamlet, nor was meant to be;
nor am I a prized promise to Salome
no head on a platter, (not that it should matter but I am neither
a Baptist nor a Basquiat.)
In fact there is no inhibition to this decision as we fall like
autumn leaves.

We have lingered in the chambers of the pubs and clubs
served by bar-girls wreathed with glitter and garlands
We have tasted the food
we have gone at dusk wept and feasted, feasted and prayed that
this was not all there is
but it was all there is
until this dish

Let the mermaids catch my fall and my abject disappointment
Let us eat
let us eat and go then, you and I
with the evening spread out against the sky
tonight we dine
this night we die.

Biographies

Abi Idowu

Abi Idowu started writing properly when she was 18 and was first published at that age. It took her a bit longer to know about men. She was introduced to cooking by her mother when as a child she tried to fry an egg with water. This poem is her first in three years and it has inspired her to create a food gallery where her cooking takes centre stage. To while away the long nights of insomnia, she makes really fabulous cards.

Adam Lowe

Adam Lowe is a writer, publisher and journalist from Leeds. He currently lives in Manchester, where he runs Young Enigma, a writer development programme for emerging LGBT writers, supported by Commonword and Arts Council England. His pamphlet *Precocious* was a reader nomination for the Guardian First Book Award. In 2012 he was Olympic poet for Yorkshire, and in 2013 he was honoured as LGBT History Month Poet Laureate. He runs Dog Horn Publishing, a publisher of cutting edge and transgressive literature.

Almira Holmes

Almira has been writing for a number of years. She writes poetry and short fiction and has been published widely. Her first published poem appeared in *Mslexia* in 2000. Almira holds degrees in English and Creative Writing and works with a number of writing groups.

Currently, Almira is working on a couple of editing projects.

Anna Percy

Anna Percy was born and educated in Norfolk. She gained a Creative Writing and Contemporary Culture BA from CIA in 2007 and a Creative Writing MA in 2009 from University of

Cumbria. She has been writing for performance and publication around the country for the best part of a decade. She is the author of three chapbooks and her first collection comes out with flapjack press in 2013. Her work errs towards free verse and increasingly the experimental and encompasses love loss losing your mind the pastoral and the surreal.

Aryamati Olga Kenyon Brooks
My Polish father left soon after my birth to devote himself to greater ideals, which I admire. My mother found herself overwhelmed by her vocal daughter and premature son. She inherited three farms, but so mismanaged the rents that we were left with a caravan in one field. She fell ill, physically and mentally, when I was 10, died when l was just 17. My adolescence was devoted to nursing her, with no training. Only recently have I felt able to write about this farcical tragedy.

Basir Sultan Kazmi
Born in Pakistan in 1953, Basir Sultan Kazmi is a poet in the ghazal tradition of his illustrious father, the late Nasir Kazmi. He taught English at the Government College Lahore. In the UK, he has taught at schools and at Bradford University. He has two Urdu poetry collections and a few plays. Translations of his ghazals have been published in several magazines and anthologies. He won the North West Playwrights Workshop Award in 1992. He has recited his poetry in several cities of Europe, as well as in Pakistan, India, UAE and the USA.

Brigid Rose
Brigid Rose is a writer and artist currently living in rural mid Wales. She writes poetry and fiction, both of which have been published in various magazines and anthologies. In 2009 her debut novel, *The City of Lists* was published by Crocus Books. Her creative pursuits are presently taking a back seat to her fierce drive to uncover the mysteries of life, the universe and everything, all of which are turning out to be a lot more incredible than she

originally thought. Examples of her artwork and writing can be viewed at www.littlefish.org.uk

Chanje Kunda

Chanje Kunda is a poet, playwright, performance artist and female emcee. She has done countless performances, gracing the likes of the Royal Albert Hall in London, Calabash Literature Festival Jamaica, ZID Theatre and Biljmepark Theatre, Amsterdam, and has featured for Apples and Snakes at Battersea Arts Centre and Soho Theatre London. She produced a Hip Hop poetry EP One Voice, for which she won Female MC Award and performed at the Urban Music Stage at the *Rise London Unite Music Festival*, which boasted some 80,000 festival goers.

Charlotte Gringras

Charlotte Gringras spent years teaching and studying, including an MA in Jewish Studies at Manchester, recently. On attending her first creative writing group, seven years ago, she was hooked immediately, subsequently joining the award-winning writing circle, Womanswrite, in Manchester. The city has nurtured her feminist tendencies and is where her attitude and her feet are firmly based; it also sets the scene for her first novel, *The Purple Rose*. Including the novel, Charlotte's writing has had some success. A short play broadcast on local radio, two short stories and over twenty poems published and encouragement from family, provide great incentive.

Cheryl Martin

After starting out as a performance poet back in the day with the likes of Segun Lee-French, Shamshad Khan, Anjum Malik, and others in the legendary original Identity workshop under Lemn Sissay, Cheryl went on to become an award-winning playwright and director — two Manchester Evening News Theatre Awards, an Edinburgh Festival Fringe First and a premiere at the very first Manchester International Festival, and counting. After numerous residencies - Ilkley Literature Festival, Birmingham

Readers and Writers Festival, Manchester Commonwealth Games Artist-in-Residence, she took a break from writing to concentrate on directing, becoming Associate Director New Writing/New Work at Contact theatre and Director-in-Residence at Edinburgh's Traverse along the way. Now it's time to get back to basics: poetry from deep in the marrow.

Chris Jam

ChriSJaM is a performance poet, Dj and radio presenter who migrated to the Mancuniverse from Londinium in 1986 at the height of the summer of love and formed the *Jam mc's:-* a sound system with a distinctive lyrical style.

In 1994, with Segun Lee French, Barney Doodlebug and with the backing of Green Room Director, Garfield Allen, Chris Jam created Speakeasy, an open mic night for spoken word artists and lyricists of all forms.

A full audio version of YabbY Yoods is available at www.soundcloud.com/chrisjam

Conor Aylward

Conor Aylward has been many things: ticket tearer, carpet fitter's lad and lighting controller. Now due to the realities of living with fibromyalgia, he only writes for his own pleasure and can occasionally be seen going to the shops for milk.

Daniella Edwards

Daniella Edwards is a poet on the rise. She has performed her work at Iguana Bar, Manchester, at Dry Bar for the Mothers Against Violence team and at a host of other locations across the UK. She has a National Diploma in Drama, a HNC in Theatre and further qualifications in Preparing To Teach in the Lifelong Learning Sector. She acted the main part in Commonword's recent, *Ghosts-Disappearing Histories* play. She runs drama workshops for young people and is developing a solo show.

Elmi Ali

Elmi is a writer/performer and facilitator based in the North West. He is part of the prestigious Young Identity poetry collective and the Inna Voice Ensemble. He writes poetry, short stories and drama. He has performed in venues across the county including Westminster, The Southbank Centre and Contact Theatre, Manchester. His work is displayed at the Royal Manchester Children's Hospital and has appeared in *Poetry Review* as well as *Scarf Magazine*, of which he is an Associate Editor. He teaches poetry and creative writing to adults and young people across the county in partnership with organisations such as the Arvon Foundation. Elmi is currently working on his first collection of poetry.

Emma Purshouse

Emma Purshouse is a writer and performance poet. She has appeared as a featured artist at various spoken word nights including Apples and Snakes' *Hit the Ode*, Birmingham and *Bang Said The Gun*, Manchester. She has undertaken writing residencies for Wolverhampton Libraries and The New Vic Theatre in Stoke-on-Trent.

Emma has been published in small press magazines and poetry anthologies. A CD of her work, entitled *Upsetting the Applecart*, was released by Offa's Press in 2010 (www.offaspress.co.uk). In 2012 she was shortlisted for the Mslexia unpublished novel prize. Emma also MCs a regular spoken word night in the West Midlands.

Fokkina McDonnell

Fokkina McDonnell lives in Manchester. She is a psychotherapist and supervisor in private practice, with a special interest in using EMDR for performance anxiety. She has been writing short stories and poems for over 15 years with work being broadcast, published in magazines, journals and anthologies in the UK and the Netherlands. Recent poems have also been shortlisted, highly commended and placed in national and international competitions, including the RedPage Sonnet Prize in the 14th Ware Open Poetry Competition. Fokkina is currently studying with Ann and Peter Sansom at the Writing School with a view to completing her first pamphlet.

Gillian Forrester
Gillian Forrester spent much of her life in bars - Stable Bar in Wigan, Two Trees on Union St in Plymouth, Carlton Hotel on Guernsey, where she kissed Oliver Reed, and the Still and West in Old Portsmouth.

After a motorbike crash brought her back to Wigan she collected some late GCSE's, acquired a BA (Hons) at Manchester Polytechnic, and wrote a collection of short stories - which is still available to buy.

The last ten years has seen her setting up and then coordinating Wigan's Words Literature Festival but she stepped down in 2012 to await a new American kneecap.

Helene Marks
Being congenitally lazy about cooking, and having run out of M&S's prepared meals one night, I realized my fridge contained only 2 eggs. Risking salmonella, they being, of course, out of date. I did indeed cook 2 eggs. I cooked the poem at the same time. Oh, if it was always so easy to conjure up a poem, I swear I would take up cooking.

Hua Zi
Born in China shortly before the ten year Cultural Revolution, she grew up and was educated in China. She loves Chinese literature and is proud of her Chinese cultural heritage, hence the name Hua Zi (from *Hua Xia Zi Sun* - meaning *the child of China*). She has studied and worked in the UK for some two decades and now lives, with her husband, in Manchester where she enjoys the

cultural and creative diversity. She often retreats to the fictional world and feels at ease there. She is most grateful for all the help and support she has received from Commonword.

Jennifer Nansubuga Makumbi

Jennifer Nansubuga Makumbi is from Uganda. She currently teaches Creative Writing at Lancaster University. Her research interests are Postcolonial literature with specific interest in African oral traditional forms, feminism and masculinities. She won the 2013 Kwani Manuscript prize with her first novel, *The Kintu Saga*, and is currently working on her second novel, *Child In The Anthill*. She has been published in African Writing Magazine and most recently in *Moss Side Stories* (Crocus 2012). The poems here are the first that she has written.

Joan Ncube

Joan Ncube is a twenty year old Manchester-based poet who has been a member of Young Identity for four years and of Sanctum for a year. She helps facilitate Young Identity workshops in Abraham Moss Library. A student of Advertising and Brand Management in Manchester, Joan has performed at Royal Exchange Theatre, South Bank and Park Life '10, and was part of a group of young poets who shared a stage with the legendary Amiri Baraka as part of Manchester Literature Festival 2012. Joan was Assistant Director in the short film, *Selective* and has been part of other creative projects. She recently took up knitting as a hobby.

Jolivia Gaston

Born in 1950 to English and Nigerian parents, at an early age I was fostered out with my twin sister in Levenshulme, Manchester. We returned to our birth mother at the age of 10. Looking back, I've been on a long journey influenced by my roots: England, Africa and America. I've been writing poetry since 2000. Small pieces of work have been published in *Rain Dog* and the Suitcase Books' *Hair* anthology. I performed at the Didsbury Art Festival in 2010.

I am a member of The Monday Night Group, Commonword and Identity. I am currently developing some new work, including children's poetry which I hope to self publish on completion.

Katie Haigh

Katie Haigh was born in August 1981. She is from Heywood, Lancashire. Although Katie has struggled with a range of physical and mental health problems since her early teenage years, she has managed to cope with raising a family. Katie has used creative writing as an outlet for her range of conditions. She performs regularly at local open mic nights and has previously been published in *Scribble* and *North West Focus*. Last year she had her first book of poetry, *Prejudice and Pride* published by Chipmunka Publishing.

Kayleigh Kavanagh

Kayleigh Kavanagh recently graduated from the University of Cumbria after studying English and Creative Writing. She experiments with various forms and repeatedly creates new and engaging material. She was an intern for Commonword, and learnt extensively from this experience. To date she has had several poems published and now through Descent Theatre, a play also. Whilst working long term on her novel, she enjoys writing other pieces.

Keisha Thompson

By the age of 16 Keisha Thompson had been published in three anthologies and had performed her work at various venues including Urbis, Contact and Bolton Octagon. In 2007, she joined Young identity poetry collective and subsequently competed in international poetry festival Brave New Voices '08 & '09. In '10 the group were privileged to perform at the renowned Nuyorican Poetry Cafe, New York. She both authored and featured in a short film, *Selective* that was screened at Cornerhouse in 2010. Most recently she performed commissioned pieces for the Amiri Baraka/Manchester Literature Festival programme and for

Apples & Snakes' 30th Anniversary. She has begun working on a solo show.

Khaleal Coleman

I used to hate writing. I found poetry interesting but could never get past the boring old stuff you learn in school. Then I went to London with Young Identity and experienced a Poetry Slam. It opened my eyes to the fun side of poetry and after a couple of sessions, I was getting published.

Lathifa Baumgartner

Lathifa Baumgartner is Singaporean and resides in Switzerland. A teacher, she specialises in teaching Young Learners. She enjoys writing at the same time and compares it to being on holiday. She has written articles for nursing newsletters and published poems in *Offshoots*, writing from Geneva and in *Writers' Works Bern*. To her, teaching and writing are twin passions. She has a Postgraduate Diploma in Creative Writing.

Laura Sinclair

Teacher, painter and writer of Jamaican decent, Laura Sinclair started writing, through diaries, at the age of 8 and has continued for twenty years. The childlike awe of the mundane shines through her picture-provoking poetry. She has performed poetry all around Manchester. Notable performances include Apples and Snakes and Royal Exchange Theatre Manchester. She has painted and exhibited for Cultureword, Back to Roots project and Didsbury Arts Festival, to name a few. She uses her gift to capture the overflow of emotions that life stirs.

Louise Fazackerley

Louise Fazackerley is a performance poet based in the North West. She graduated from Lancaster University with a 2:1 in Theatre Studies and Creative Writing before turning her back on all things creative and embracing all things social. Louise has worked in the NHS, in children's homes, as a careers advisor and as a library manager before realising you can change the world with spoken word. Her work is displayed in the Olympic Park and on Wigan Wallgate train station. She loves: running workshops, working with children and young people, libraries, poetry slams, festivals and being outside. Twitter @louisethepoet

Louise Wallwein

Louise Wallwein is a poet/playwright. Her career took off in 1998 when she performed a legendary one-woman show on the wing of a Shackleton aircraft in the Manchester Museum of Science and Industry. She has had plays commissioned by Contact Theatre, Arena Theatre Company Australia, Sydney Opera House, Red Ladder Theatre Company, the BBC, Royal Exchange Theatre and Sheffield Crucible. Louise Wallwein has conducted many Poetry Residencies. In 2006 she became Poet in Residence of Queensland, Australia. She is very proud of her work in communities, and has worked with thousands of people, helping them to find and develop their voice.

Lynn Walton

I have been writing since the age of ten, inspired by the fact one of my poems got published in the Manchester Evening News. As a "grown up" I have been published by Writers' Bureau, Beehive Press, Virago Press, and Crocus. More recently I have had poems accepted by Best of Manchester Poets and the Poetry Box where my dark and Gothic writings are regularly published. For relaxation, I like to write poems about the untimely demise of my husband. I perform these at local clubs, and find this keeps him on his toes!

Mark Mace Smith

Mark Mace Smith was born to Ackee and Saltfish in Battersea in 1973. Schooled on fish & chips, spam and roly-poly until 1995, he moved north to parched peas, barm cakes and butter pies to study philosophy and politics.

In 2008, unable to stomach journalism (or Preston) Mark

graduated to masticating Manchester Puddings, gobbling Eccles Cakes and quaffing Vimto in the salubriously appetising suburb of Whalley D'Range.

Mark cooks up poetry to a family recipe of dub reggae, hip-hop and classical music blended with slave songs, dystopian realities and existential anarchy. Politically simmering. Spiritually bubbling. Best served hot and FRESH!

Meshach R. Brencher

I first started writing poetry in 2009, while studying a Visual Art course and producing performance art work. My style is written using a persona, with a split personality as I touch on subjects, which are deep and thought-provoking or dry humour and other crazy scenarios. I suffer from learning and processing disabilities so it literally influences a complex flow of my structure, whether I produce free verse or lyrical poems following rhythm. My favourite style of poetry is Romanticism, which focuses on natural, emotional and personal themes to the words. I feel it best reflects my way of writing.

Nabila Jameel

Nabila Jameel is a British Pakistani poet, working and living in Manchester. Her poems have been published by Stand magazine, the Poetry Review and in a recent anthology by Bloodaxe, *Out of Bounds*. She taught English in the further education sector and now works for a publisher. She recently contributed a chapter for an academic book discussing the importance of performance for all writers and is currently working on her first poetry collection, which is a series of critical snapshots of society.

Nadeem Zafar

Nadeem Zafar is a poet/singer-songwriter from Manchester. In February 2001 he began his performance poetry career at The Green Room in Manchester. He has had his writing featured in two anthologies of poetry, two poetry magazines, and on various websites. He also acts as an unofficial mentor for new writers via Commonword's renowned Identity workshop which he has attended since July 2005.

Neil McCall

I have been a member of Commonword's Monday Night Group for several years. I live in South Manchester, work in the financial industry (boo!) and am counting down to retiring next year (hooray!). Besides poetry events, I enjoy birdwatching, travel, curries, good beer and rock music, and my wife occasionally drags me out on a healthy geocaching ramble as an antidote to the last three. Cake has sadly been reduced from a staple food source to an occasional treat.

Rachel Halsall

Rachel Halsall is an eighteen year old writer, part-time model and full time college student who has a great love of art in all forms, but in particular the literary kind. She wrote her first poem when she was five years old and has been writing ever since. Rachel has been published several times in teen anthologies and is currently working on a number of horror stories, a genre with which she is deeply enamoured. She is also active in and writes articles for the alternative feminist community, Mookychick.

Reece Williams

Reece is a poet, a member of Young Identity & Inna Voice collectives, a peer mentor, a workshop facilitator and an aspiring theatre producer. Currently studying Music, Theatre and Entertainment Management at The Liverpool Institute for Performing Arts (LIPA), Reece has a particular interest in modern and innovative literature and theatre. Having experienced first-hand the transforming effect that participation in the arts can have, he is passionate about helping young people develop as artists.

revporl

Originally from the swamps of Stockport, Paul "Rev Porl" Stevens has been performing as a poet since 1995. The main thrust of his work has been to bring poetry to non-poetry audiences, usually by appearing as a compere or support act to bands playing at venues such as Night and Day, the Star and Garter, Retro Bar and the Roadhouse. He has supported veteran Punk bands the UK Subs, GBH and the Subhumans, has appeared with Attilla the Stockbroker and Nick Toczek and has performed throughout most of England and Wales bearing sharp shades, a pint of something lethal and a big pink cross. 2012 saw the launch of *Rise of Neon*, his début novella, the first in a series of Superhero books set in Manchester.

Sarah Gbeleyi

After a stint in film, tv and radio broadcast, followed by a bit of technical theatre, I am finally focusing on the two things I like most, education and arts admin. I am currently training as a teacher. I have been writing for over fifteen years but have only begun to share my work in the last three years. I use writing as creative catharsis to process thought and emotion, I also enjoy the challenge of responding to creative briefs. The food anthology allowed me to do this, combining food and creative writing to make an appetizing treat.

Sheree Mack

Sheree Mack is a freelance writer focusing on the science of memory while writer in residence at the Lit and Phil in Newcastle. *Family Album* (2011) is her first collection with Flambard Press. *Laventille* will be out in 2015 with Smokestack Books. She has a PhD in black British women's poetry.

Shirley May

Shirley May has performed extensively at prominent venues across the North West and has been published in numerous anthologies. She is currently working on her one woman show,

So Here I Am. She has extensive experience in developing creative writing programmes for youth services, libraries, and arts organisations. As a poet and facilitator she works regularly in schools and Young Offender institutions.

Shirley Percy

Shirley Percy retired from the Manchester Schools Ethnic Minority learning Support Service eight years ago. Since then she has pursued her interest in Buddhism and become a member of the Triratna community. She has enjoyed using the freedom of retirement to write poems and short stories and has been published by Blinking Eye, Norwich Writers' Circle, Ragged Raven and Best of Manchester Poets. Recently Bridge House have accepted a Science Fiction story. Shirley lives in Bury with her husband and three (ex stray) cats.

Shoeless Carole

I live in North West England, I work as a nurse and have recently completed a degree in medical herbalism. I have many and varied interests, and one of these is poetry. In the last few years I have taken to writing about subjects that reflect on life and its varied events. This poem was written following a challenge from a close friend to write a poem using the Fibonacci sequence of numbers. I chose to write about the raspberry that grows in this natural formation so common to many plants and animals in the natural world.

Steve Garside

Steve Garside is a painter, photographer, poet and writer. He has exhibited his work in the UK and Europe, and has had poetry published in the UK, USA and Europe.

SuAndi

SuAndi was born in Hulme, Manchester. She writes mainly for performance. Her work is crafted to 'sound like a conversation [...] my mother's mouth was filled with the over-the-fence chatter of Liverpool, expanding her expressions with an inherited Irish superstitiousness - we never did anything that might tempt fate against us. So we never wrote anything down, preferring to whisper it on.'

Since 1985 she has expanded her portfolio of work into diverse locations, from galleries to public artwork. She is the freelance Cultural Director of National Black Arts Alliance, a recipient of a NESTA Dreamtime award, and in 1999 she was awarded an OBE in the Queen's Honours list for her contributions to the Black Arts Sector. She is one of four Honorary Creative Writing Fellows for Leicester University's School of English.

Sue Stern

Sue Stern was born in London but has lived in Manchester since she was five. She has always written - diaries, stories, plays in French for the children she taught - until the discovery of Commonword in the nineties, inspired her to write seriously. She has published poems and short fiction in Britain and America, and has an MA in writing children's fiction (MMU). Deeply affected by her radical upbringing: grandparents, Russian, Jewish anarchists, parents, committed socialists, sometime fellow travellers, she has explored themes of alienation in her work. She has recently set up her fledgling imprint, Red Bank Books, to publish *Rafi Brown and the Candy Floss Kid*, a novel for children aged 8-11.

Tia McHale

I was born in June 2000. I like chilling with friends, shopping, playing netball and rugby, attending army cadets and listening to music. I have two pet rottweilers called Samson and Roxy, which I love very much. My favourite hobby is writing poetry. I enjoy writing because it is a great way to describe your thoughts and feelings. I have another poem published with Young Writers. Someday I hope to write my own book.

Tony Walsh

Tony Walsh, aka Longfella, is "one of the UK's leading voices in performance poetry" (StAnza International Poetry Festival). He performs his poetry at literary and music festivals around the UK and beyond, and leads acclaimed workshops in schools, colleges, universities and prisons. His work has been commissioned by BBC television and radio, published in magazines and anthologies in both the UK and USA, and recently translated into Russian as part of EnglishPEN's Pussy Riot campaign. Tony's debut full collection *SEX & LOVE & ROCK&ROLL* was published in Spring 2013 by Burning Eye. www.longfella.co.uk @LongfellaPoet

Winston Plowes

Winston Plowes composes his poetry with his two cats on a narrowboat in Hebden Bridge. He hopes to make people pause and ponder the hidden details of life. He has recently enjoyed correspondence with World Trade Centre architect Daniel Libeskind and ceramicist Gordon Baldwin after writing about their work; and with the local butcher who enjoyed his poem 'A sonnet to bacon' and slipped an extra rasher into his order. His collection of ghazals *First of all I Wrote Your Name* will be published by Stairwell Books in 2013. www.winstonplowes. co.uk

Yusra Warsama

Yusra Warsama is a performance poet, actor, writer and theatre practitioner. Her passions lie in creating work through play and exploration of life experiences in the world we live in. Past, present and future work takes many forms, from her developing a one woman show which uses spoken word, storytelling, live art and physical expression, to 'Grace' (05) and 'Make – Believe' (09) with Quarantine, which looks at exploring theatre without focus on characters but instead on the one to one relationship between performer and audience.

Yusra is writing a play for the Birmingham Repertory

Theatre with two other writers. She is also filming her second international feature and tutoring at the Royal Court London.

Yvonne McCalla

The 'bass chasing dub talking deep seeing' poet, Yvonne McCalla is one of Manchester's finest poets. "As a little girl I'd get this itch in my hand, which required a pen and paper and ended up with me writing. Sometimes I don't even know what I'm going to write but when I get that itch I know something is on its way!" Yvonne has been curator of Commonword's recent, Moss Side Stories/Disappearing Histories project; poet facilitator for Wordsmith Awards schools creative writing project, and poet-coach/performer at Speakeasy Exodus festival, Royal Exchange Theatre. Her poems have featured on the **International Museum of Women** website & online exhibition *Exhibiting You*, San Francisco, and on Manchester's *Rainy City* website.

Zodwa Nyoni

Zodwa Nyoni is a Zimbabwean-born live artist, poet and playwright. She's had writing residencies at Leeds Kirkgate Market (2012), I Love West Leeds festival (2010) and BBC Radio Leeds (2006). She's been commissioned by West Yorkshire Playhouse for Leeds Light Night (2012) and Transform Festival (2013). Zodwa has written four plays that have showcased at the Leeds Metropolitan University, Leeds University, Theatre in the Mill, Square Chapel, West Yorkshire Playhouse and The Bush Theatre. She has performed her poetry at the British Museum, Ilkely Literature Festival, Bridlington Literature Festival, Southbank Centre, Bush Theatre and Nuyorican Poets Café (New York City). Her poetry is featured in the *Suitcase Book of Love Poems, Sable Lit Magazine, The Warehouse Magazine* (Canada) and Aesthetica Magazine's *Creative Works Annual 2009*.